Building Cloud Native Apps Painlessly

The Prescriptive Guide to

Kubernetes and Jenkins X

Robert Davies

Brian Dawson

James Rawlings

James Strachan

Published by

HURWITZ
& ASSOCIATES
Insight to Action

Building Cloud Native Apps Painlessly
The Prescriptive Guide to Kubernetes and Jenkins X

By Robert Davies, Brian Dawson, James Rawlings and
James Strachan

Published by
Hurwitz & Associates, LLC
35 Highland Circle
Needham, MA 02494

ISBN: 978-1-949260-12-0

Printed in the USA by Hurwitz & Associates, LLC
www.hurwitz.com

Acknowledgments

This book has been a collaboration between the authors, publisher and editors. Some of the team members that helped make this book possible are:

Managing Editors:
Judith Hurwitz, Hurwitz & Associates
Daniel Kirsch, Hurwitz & Associates

Editorial Project Manager: Diana Hwang, CloudBees, Inc.

Cover and Graphic Design: Kate Myers

Layout and Interior Design: Caroline Wilson

Table of Contents

About the Authors

Robert Davies
Robert is the vice president of engineering at CloudBees, Inc. He joined CloudBees from Red Hat to co-create the Jenkins X initiative. Rob was the creator of ActiveMQ and has worked on open source initiatives for over 10 years.

Brian Dawson
Brian is currently a DevOps evangelist and practitioner at CloudBees, Inc. with a focus on agile, continuous integration (CI), continuous delivery (CD) and DevOps practices. He has over 25 years as a software professional in multiple domains including quality assurance, engineering and management, with a focus on optimization of software development. Brian has led an agile transformation consulting practice and helped many organizations implement CI, CD and DevOps.

James Rawlings
James is a principal software engineer for CloudBees, Inc. and co-created the Jenkins X project. James is a lead developer, frequent blogger and aims to help developers move to the cloud. James was formally at Red Hat and worked on the fabric8 project.

James Strachan
James is a distinguished engineer at CloudBees, Inc. and chief architect of Jenkins X. He is also the founder of the Apache Groovy programming language, Apache Camel and co-founder of Apache ServiceMix and fabric8. James is a frequent speaker and blogger on Jenkins X. He is actively involved with the Kubernetes, developer tool and continuous delivery open source communities. Before joining CloudBees, James worked at Red Hat and FuseSource.

Preface

A LETTER FROM THE CREATOR OF JENKINS

When I wrote the first line of a shell script that would eventually become Jenkins, one of the motivations was to make myself and other developers in the team more productive. Software development in my team was still held together in good part by lots of manual work, emails, meetings and phone calls. I felt like a bit of automation would go a long way in reducing those, so that we could all spend more time doing things that actually matter, such as designing, collaborating and writing more code.

That shell script is long gone, but it turns out the idea lived longer than any of the code written for Jenkins, and got bigger than myself. It transcended beyond me to the Jenkins community of thousands of contributors and millions of users. It took me time to understand what was really going on, but it turns out there were a lot of people like me everywhere in the world. Under the umbrella of the Jenkins project, we were able to join hands - developer to developer - to collectively create this open source ecosystem that enabled us to build amazing applications faster.

And it's this same idea that carries through to Jenkins X, the newest addition to the Jenkins family. Jenkins X takes a bold and exciting approach to this idea. It takes all the "awesome" (which is one of the James Strachan-isms I picked up) things happening in the world of microservices and cloud native application development and assembles those into a simple form that makes sense for everyone.

This is great because the technology landscape of web application development is evolving at a breakneck speed, and that's forcing everyone to pause and understand how to effectively utilize the latest additions to their toolbox. Kubernetes, twelve factor apps, environment provisioning, horizontal scaling ... the list goes on. It's almost as if what's supposed to make you productive is actually slowing you down.

That's why we built Jenkins X. It takes all those concerns and bottlenecks out of the process. It makes the easiest thing the right thing, so that you can focus on what matters.

And above all, we built Jenkins X because we are driven by the basic human desire to help others. Indeed, people in the Jenkins community take great pride and satisfaction in helping you, our fellow software developers. So please take this little gift from us. I know you will like it.

Kohsuke Kawaguchi
Creator of Jenkins, CTO of CloudBees, Inc.

Introduction

We are entering a new era where developers need to begin building cloud native applications based on a container-ized, microservices architecture. At the same time, there has been an incredible amount of innovation based on the open source revolution. This innovation is driving change in the world of software development and deployment at a frenetic pace. When executed well, these new applications will help businesses be better prepared for changes in customer requirements.

The purpose of this book is to introduce you to the com-bination of two powerful open source standards: Kuber-netes and Jenkins X. Kubernetes is the de facto standard for container orchestration while Jenkins X is a platform that hides the complexities of Kubernetes from the devel-oper. By adopting Jenkins X, developers are able to focus on creating high-quality code and excellent user experi-ences rather than getting bogged down by the intricacies of Kubernetes.

The power of Kubernetes and Jenkins X together, is a partnership that enables organizations to leverage cloud native environments in a consistent and predictable way. To be successful in a cloud dominated world requires that teams of business and technical leaders collaborate to create meaningful solutions to make customers success-ful. This collaboration results in new business models that can change the way business is revolutionized.

Why read this book?

This book gives you a roadmap to understanding what Ku-bernetes is and the ecosystem of open source tools that sur-round it. We will put this important platform in context with cloud native applications and continuous integration and continuous deployment. You will learn what it is like to create new, cloud native applications and the emerging new challenges. Once you understand the complexities inherent in containers and container orchestration, along with an appreciation of the hundreds of open source tools, it will become clear that an environment like Jenkins X has the potential to change everything. The book will discuss the building blocks to Jenkins X and will give you a prescriptive guidance on how to get started.

Who should read this book?

This book is written for developers and DevOps managers who are beginning to understand the power of open source tools such as Kubernetes and Jenkins X, and give you insights into the new world of cloud native applications development. Both developers and operations teams need to understand continuous integration and continuous delivery in order to be successful. We wrote this book so that you can share your insights and observations with your management team and your colleagues to support the goals of modern application development and deployment.

This book is not documentation nor is it a technical manual, but it gives you a framework to understand your next steps in creating true business value. Future books in this series will delve deeper into the details of leveraging Jenkins X to support your cloud native applications development and deployment. It is important to remember that Jenkins X is a community project and it will continue to evolve to meet the changing needs of contributors, developers and customers.

Chapter 1
Transitioning to Modern Application Development

Inside

» The impact of modern applications on customer engagement

» Cashing in on the cloud

» The evolution of DevOps

» Building security into your development process

» The increasing importance of clouds, containers and microservices

Software has become the critical tool driving businesses forward in new and innovative ways. Applications have never been more important and the relationship between many businesses and their customers is solely based around mobile and web applications. Application performance, quality, and user experience is critical. To create a competitive advantage, businesses are taking a new approach to software development and delivery. This modern approach to application development demands changes to culture, process and technology. Continuous integration, continuous delivery, distributed team, DevOps, microservices and cloud first are all emerging as critical elements for organizations that want to transform their development and deployment organizations.

The new generation of software development demands collaboration between developers, operations and security professionals. Keeping pace with the fast speed business change and innovation requires flexibility, agility and teamwork across business and technical teams. In this chapter, we will discuss how the demands of modern applications development drive the transition to the cloud and impact cloud development.

Impact of next generation development and deployment

Modern application development addresses two key issues - legacy tools that make it difficult for globally distributed teams to collaborate and organizational silos. Firstly, modern application development decentralizes many tasks in the development and deployment chain. Software services can be developed across the globe and may involve multiple teams each working on a portion of an application. Secondly, there is a need to break down silos across departments within the business. While this decentralized model may seem to be contradictory, the software development revolution taking place today provides developers with the freedom and agility to innovate with a focus on business goals, rather than organizational or functional silos even though teams may be geographically dispersed.

Over the past decade, organizations have moved to a cloud-based IT infrastructure to reduce cost, lower administration overhead and gain flexibility. The early transition to the cloud was mostly focused on costs, however. Today, companies now look to the cloud for a strategic advantage. The cloud gives teams rapid access to a scalable infrastructure that can support a new model of development. The economic benefits of the cloud – in the forms of lower costs, reduced capital investment, and greater flexibility - are undeniable. Yet the growing adoption of the cloud among organizations also change both the development and deployment landscapes. For instance, when hybrid clouds and/or multiple public clouds are involved, or a single monolithic architecture is decomposed into cloud-based microservices, creating and managing applications and data can turn into very complicated tasks.

Developers and IT managers will need new tools and capabilities to effectively navigate this terrain. They will need to review and analyze their current datacenters and policies, the relationship among IT, business units, and executive management, and how these factors affect IT decisions. And, more importantly, IT leaders need to reevaluate their current development and deployment practices. They must assess how all of the business and IT stakeholders work together and the processes, tools and technology that can help modernize their business.

Forward-looking IT leaders ask questions about how they can create agile and advanced approaches to customer engagement to implement new innovative strategies. They look at new development approaches, and new deployment and delivery models, from cross-functional agile teams using cloud-based tools to highly decomposed and distributed applications. In short, insightful developers are moving away from developing monolithic code and applications to creating standards-based business services incorporating agile code and a microservices architecture. These services can be linked together to create business value. This is becoming the new normal.

Modern applications – customer focused and demand driven

Market changes and intensifying competitive forces introduce a set of dynamics requiring businesses to adjust in order to stay competitive. These, in turn, drive the changes we see today in how software is developed and managed as businesses move at an accelerated pace.

What does this increased competition mean for software development? It requires agility and a software architecture developed and delivered with speed and precision. It means software can and will change frequently as the business needs, and competitive and technological landscape changes. It means that when code is changed, it is then automatically tested, and vetted in small increments. It means services are isolated from the underlying platform, and are independently built by small teams using common tools and development practices. It means that each service will be delivered on an immutable infrastructure using containers - fast, stable and in direct response to needs of the business, market, and most importantly the end-user.

As more and more customers rely on next generation mobile and web applications to execute and manage transactions (purchases, correspondences, shopping, etc.), businesses need to make the customer experience as efficient and satisfying as possible. This means customer facing systems must be easy to use; provide access to all functions and capabilities relevant at any point in time. It must be transparent and integrate with other core services such as billing, sales, etc. All of the services, no matter where they physically reside, need to work together seamlessly. However, there must be a high degree of flexibility so necessary changes can be executed quickly as customer expectations change and competitive threats emerge.

Economic incentives of the cloud

While we continually talk about innovation and differentiation, costs considerations are top of mind with business management. This is especially true as businesses rely even more on IT to help them differentiate their business and offer a competitive advantage.

IT continues to be called upon to "do more with less" in order to build the applications a business requires and to maintain and enhance assets already in products to offer a competitive advantage. Keeping these "development-focused" IT costs in control requires new, more efficient ways to develop applications, modernize existing applications, and manage the environment to ensure high availability and performance. The potentially higher complexity resulting from a more modular, distributed deployment approach, and rapid changes in market and competitive conditions to which developers must respond, requires new methodologies and tools to support development efforts. But costs go beyond how developers do their jobs. Many companies, facing the need to expand their IT presence with more systems, storage, and other assets, may quickly find their costs can outstrip their budget.

One way to cut costs is to adopt affordable public cloud services that make it possible to implement changes quickly and scale up and down depending on a business' changing needs.

Achieving enterprise agility

The new generation of agile application development and deployment means software services can be developed and deployed virtually anywhere. Microservices enable applications to be developed as services linked together through lightweight interfaces. Each service can be developed and deployed by small independent teams. This flexibility provides greater benefits in terms of performance, cost and scalability. This approach of building services, packaging them together and managing them consistently and predictably, demands a new approach to software development and deployment.

Lean, agile development

New approaches to software development focus on what is commonly referred to as continuous integration and continuous delivery (CI/CD). Continuous integration focuses on continuously integrating and validating changes, to code and environments to ensure errors are identified and fixed as they are introduced. In contrast, continuous delivery automates the software delivery process (non-functional testing, functional testing, security, deployment, etc.), ensuring that with each change, the application is release ready.

CI/CD allows developers to quickly identify defects as they are introduced so they can be corrected as soon as possible. When application defects are identified close to when they are introduced, it is much faster and cheaper to correct versus having to go back and reexamine the entire application. CD is in effect an extension of CI that focuses on the process of delivering changes after they are "committed" as part of the CI process. In other words, software code that passes automated tests can be considered ready for production. Continuous delivery is often used interchangeably with continuous deployment, in which all changes are automatically released to production.

Continuous integration and continuous delivery will be discussed at greater length in Chapter 2. However, if CI/CD is going to be effectively supported, it must be recognized that the two major steps in application development – development and deployment – cannot be separated as they were when employing traditional development models. This is the foundational concept behind the DevOps movement.

The new era of DevOps

DevOps is a set of cultural principles focused on aligning development and operations (and other stakeholders) around the shared objective of delivering quality software rapidly and reliably. The DevOps culture focuses on collaboration, and is an extension of agile principles. Rather than defining a rigid methodology or set of development processes, DevOps is focused on breaking down silos between teams. This new era relies on a combination of tools and best practices to accelerate the pace of application creation and enhancement.

The DevOps culture provides organizations a variety of benefits that make it a good match for today's IT environments. The most obvious is greater quality, resulting from the use of CI/CD concepts that find and correct defects early. The use of automation as a mechanism for operating and managing infrastructure and development processes makes "managing at scale" more effective. Finally, applications can be developed, changed, and delivered much faster, enabling a faster response to competitive conditions and potentially lowering costs.

DevOps is one more recent manifestation of an approach to software development known as agile, the principles of which are related to a number of software development frameworks (examples include Scrum and Kanban). The collaborative foundation of DevOps – the focus on cross-functional teams that self-organize and include end users of the software – grew out of these fundamental agile concepts. When agile principles are adopted, individual stakeholders and their interactions through collaboration are more important than adhering to strict methodologies and highly structured tools. The emphasis on speed and agility as a means to respond to rapid change brings the resulting software to the forefront, even if rigorously documenting every process step has to be put on the back burner. Being agile also means the customer – the user of the development effort's resulting product – is more of a development partner than someone to whom an invoice is sent.

Security at the forefront

Security is, for obvious reasons one of the most important considerations when developing applications for today's IT environments. Historically, the data center provided a secure platform at its core, but with a highly distributed software development environment, security now must be considered from the start of the development process. As more IT organizations change their software development practices to a more agile approach, there is no guarantee security mechanisms will be in place to provide protection for the new generation of applications. Security cannot be an afterthought, but rather needs to be built into the new software development methodologies at the beginning of the software creation process.

Despite the continued adoption of DevOps processes, unfortunately security is still often handled traditionally. In many cases, this means that, contrary to the philosophy of a DevOps approach, security is implemented sometime within, or even at the end, of a DevOps process as opposed to being embedded in the development process at the beginning. A solution to this issue is a discipline known as DevSecOps. In brief, DevSecOps is the process of integrating security into the software development process. DevSecOps begins with a change in culture founded in ongoing learning (to raise security awareness with developers who may already be entrenched in DevOps processes), the identification of security-savvy people within the organization who can champion the change in the security approach, and the empowerment of those working on security to determine how best to embed robust security into the clouds they support. Tools can then be used to automate security testing, detect vulnerabilities early, and raise security as a gate to blocking forward progress, and even the deployment of a release, if problems are found.

Cloud, containers and microservices

The change in how the industry approaches software development can be attributed to the advent of cloud computing and the availability of features and capabilities offered by cloud providers and tool vendors. In many cases, developers create applications that functionally span an organization's data center, one or more public clouds, and a variety of platforms and deployment models. With the advent of containerization, for example, applications can be deployed virtually anywhere.

The cloud has therefore given rise to a variety of architectures and technologies developers need to use, and tools that support their use. Microservices, as an example, can facilitate the development of large, complex applications by breaking them down into a set of loosely coupled services. Each service can be developed by a relatively small team of developers - or even a single developer - allowing for parallel development that can make the process more efficient and development time shorter in addition to simplifying testing. Microservices in a very real sense serves as an enabler of CI/CD.

The decentralized, modular architecture that characterize many cloud-based implementations have also encouraged the adoption of containers. Containers provide a means of packaging applications such that they are abstracted from their runtime environments. Developers can now spend their energies on creating the application logic and dependencies. Operations can focus only on how and where the logic is deployed and how it is managed without worrying about version numbers and application-specific configuration issues. Containers build on the virtualization concept by virtualizing at the operating system level, allowing for a container – or many containers - to run directly on top of the operating system kernel.

These technology advances are driving the following three cornerstones of modern software development. As depicted in Figure 1-1, these cornerstones are:

- **Standards-based tools** that can support highly distributed and flexible architectures based on the hybrid cloud.

- **The use of microservices, containers and standard APIs** to provide a consistent way to achieve modularity and service orientation.

- **Orchestration and management of services** that support flexible deployment and predictable performance and reliability. The orchestration of the various facets of automating the deployment, operations, and scaling of containers across an environment consisting of clusters of host systems can pose significant challenges.

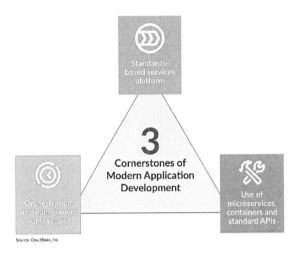

Figure 1-1: The cornerstones of modern app development

Streamlining modern application development

Modern application development requires new thinking, new platforms and tools. Without a CI/CD approach supported by important standards such as Kubernetes, teams will be bogged down in complexity. Therefore, most organizations consider Kubernetes, a standard container orchestration platform, as a good way to meet these challenges. In simple terms, Kubernetes is an open source container orchestration system for automation of the tasks mentioned above and will be covered in greater depth in Chapter 4 of this book.

One of the difficulties, however, in implementing Kubernetes is that it represents what is in essence a "blank sheet of paper" to developers who build and deploy CI/CD focused applications. Many developers are not yet very familiar with how best to create these applications on Kubernetes.

To be successful, developers need automation to be able to sustain the speed and agility required for modern software development. The Jenkins X project was initiated to address this issue by providing an automation and abstraction of the complexities of Kubernetes-native CI/CD platform to help create cloud-native applications. When integrated with Kubernetes, Jenkins X helps developers adopt Kubernetes much more easily. Chapters 5 through 7 of this book will provide a deep dive into Jenkins X.

Chapter 2

The Importance of CI/CD in the DevOps Era

Inside

> » Shifting to a continuous everything culture
> » The role of an opinionated continuous delivery pipeline
> » The importance of culture when implementing DevOps
> » Confronting the challenges of CI/CD in the cloud

Colliding forces are dramatically impacting the world of software development. Increasingly, businesses are defining their value and brand based on customer applications rather than employee-to-customer interactions and fueling the engine of their internal operations with software versus a manual process. For new businesses to succeed, and for established companies to maintain and grow their position, software development must become the center of the universe. This new model of software development requires the combination of continuous development speed, agility to change business processes, and a predictable approach to management and security. In this chapter, we will explore the growing importance of continuous integration and continuous delivery as the foundation for application development and deployment.

Defining CI/CD

While continuous integration and continuous deployment are linked together as though they were a single practice, it is important to understand both of these processes separately. This section will explain the two processes, how they relate to each other, and their value in dynamic application development, delivery and deployment.

First, we need to understand the four pillars of what is often called continuous everything. Below in Figure 2-1 is a graphic representing the continuous everything methodology.

Source: CloudBees Inc.

Figure 2-1: A methodology for approaching CI/CD

Continuous integration

Continuous integration is a software development practice in which developers frequently commit source code changes to a central repository, and the changes are continuously built and validated. This differs from the traditional development process where changes to the code might not be integrated until right before a planned release or at the end of the development cycle.

Continuous integration saves time and increases quality because errors are immediately uncovered, closer to the point they were introduced, allowing them to be corrected earlier and more easily.

Continuous testing

To meet the goal of continuous everything, a new approach to testing is needed. Testing should no longer be thought of as a stop along the delivery pipeline. Instead, testing must be an automated part of the continuous delivery pipeline. By continually testing, you can spot and remedy potential problems at the earliest possible point.

Continuous delivery

Continuous delivery extends continuous integration principles and practices further downstream in the software delivery process. With each change, continuously testing and deploying code ensures that software is in a release-ready state. Continuous delivery enables changes to be moved into pre-production or production environments, and eventually into the hands of users, in a rapid, repeatable and reliable way. Table 2-1 below provides an overview of continuous delivery.

THE BASICS OF CONTINUOUS DELIVERY
» Execute a build based on code extracted from a version control repository.
» Deploy code to the target infrastructure.
» Execute the automated steps involved in standing up or bringing down the infrastructure.
» Initiate test and rollback environments if a failure occurs.
» Log the states of code delivery.
» Provide alerts on the state of code delivery.

Source: CloudBees, Inc.

Table 2-1: The steps in achieving continuous delivery

Continuous deployment

Continuous deployment is a process where software code changes are automatically deployed into pre-production or production staging. Continuous deployment requires that there is automation along each step of the delivery pipeline.

The role of opinionated continuous delivery

Starting from scratch with CI/CD is a difficult proposition. As the adoption of continuous delivery practices increases at a rapid pace, there is a growing demand for simple solutions that allow developers and development teams to get started quickly. These fast, quick-start solutions provide an "opinion" on how continuous delivery should be achieved.

An opinionated solution serves as a starting point for teams, without the need for developers to get slowed down by complexity of process design and custom pipelines. An opinionated solution is also attractive to small teams and organizations with limited staff or expertise. These smaller, more lean teams need to focus on delivering value, not building and maintaining custom pipelines.

As we have already noted, continuous delivery is ideally built on a foundation of microservices, containers and other elements that make it possible to modularize applications for flexible deployment across multiple environments including the cloud. It's important to note that while cloud native applications are where the industry is going, existing assets (applications, tools, and systems) will continue to be part of the mix with which new applications must interact.

Once of the most challenging tasks in implementing continuous delivery, is determining the ideal workflow, including integrations, SCM strategy, environments, gates, etc. This requires a deep knowledge, multiple iterations and manual scripting. What if developers had a tool that could detect a project's type, and then build a pipeline automatically? What if a developer did not have to directly interact with Kubernetes to deploy an application to a particular environment, but rather have a tool automate that step for them? These are some examples of how the right Kubernetes platform can in effect make orchestration decisions for developers, freeing them to focus on creating business value through IT.

Challenges to CI/CD adoption

Despite the obvious advantages and benefits, there are some obstacles to adopting continuous delivery. Some of these obstacles involve human factors, while others are more technical and involve both the legacy of an organization's technology base, and the tools they use to build and deploy applications.

Change always involves risk – or at least a perception of risk. IT likely has processes and techniques in place to build applications, many of which, while manual, represent a known and comfortable approach. The benefits are obvious, but the path to adoption is not comfortable. This discomfort may also be reflected in a skills gap and the time and effort involved in bridging that gap can often be seen as a distraction from what developers know are their deliverables.

Additionally, those involved in the software development and delivery process, who are invested in manual steps and gates, often see risk in trusting these steps to automation. Even with the promise of modern approaches and practices, such as microservices and CD, technology, tools, and more importantly, culture can stand in the way.

Continuous delivery and the importance of a DevOps culture

We have described the process of continuous integration, delivery and deployment. While these practices are recognized as required components of today's face-paced, highly competitive, software-driven market, they require organization-wide changes to how software development and delivery is approached.

DevOps, a combination of the terms "development" and "operations," is an approach to software development and delivery that emphasizes a culture of collaboration to deliver software rapidly, reliably and repeatedly. DevOps is an extension of the agile movement and although it is focused on culture, a major component of DevOps is automation. Achieving the transformation to a DevOps culture requires collaboration and orchestration between all stakeholders, including development, deployment, operations and business teams.

The mandate for security

Security must be an integral part of the DevOps process. Therefore, it is not surprising to see the emergence of DevSecOps as discussed in Chapter 1. This approach brings the IT security team into the DevOps process. Rather than having an application security team review an application after it has been developed, a DevSecOps methodology integrates the security into every step of the process.

Defining the DevOps culture

Organizations have discovered through trial and error that a DevOps culture does not just happen. The process of creating the level of teamwork and collaboration requires these teams spend the time to build a culture that breaks down technical and organizational silos. Successful organizations have discovered a set of best practices for DevOps which includes a focus on outcome, the ability to continuously innovate, delivery value and learning from customer input.

The challenge of CI/CD in the cloud era

The challenge of creating collaboration between application development and deployment has been an issue for decades but the rapid growth of the cloud as a foundation for modern software development has upped the sense of urgency. Innovative IT leaders understand the only path to success is through the use of cloud native applications supported by containers and microservices. The mandate for cloud native applications, containers and microservices can only be successfully implemented with CI/CD based on a DevOps culture.

Chapter 3

Cloud Native Applications

Inside

- » Defining cloud native applications
- » Understanding the foundational architecture
- » The technology building blocks for cloud native applications
- » Preparing your company for modern app development

It should come as no surprise that an increasing number of businesses leverage cloud computing to support the speed and change necessary to stay competitive and support their customers and partners. As companies continue to invest in the cloud infrastructure, IT leaders are discovering it is not enough to simply move applications and services to the cloud. There needs to be a concerted and well-planned approach that marries the flexibility of the cloud with the requirement for continuous integration and continuous delivery discussed in Chapter 2.

The industry has done a good job of creating a scalable computing infrastructure. However, the real value for organizations moving forward is the transition to cloud native applications. In this chapter, we explain what cloud native applications are and their importance in creating an agile development and deployment environment.

Defining cloud native applications

As the cloud matures and becomes more sophisticated, it too, evolves to support the way cloud applications are defined. This brings us to the value of cloud native applications. In brief, cloud native applications are software offerings designed with microservices, containers and dynamic orchestration as well as continuous delivery of software. Every part of the cloud native application is housed within its own container and dynamically orchestrated with other containers to optimize the way resources are utilized.

Taking a step back, the concept of cloud native changes the way we think about application creation and management. The Cloud Native Computing Foundation, an organization founded in 2015 under the auspices of the Linux Foundation, "builds sustainable ecosystems and fosters a community around a constellation of high-quality projects that orchestrate containers as part of a microservices architecture." The Cloud Native Computing Foundation defines cloud native as follows:

- **Container packaged.** A standard way to package applications that is resource efficient. More applications can be densely packed using a standard container format.

- **Dynamically managed.** A standard way to discover, deploy and scale up and down containerized applications.

- **Microservices oriented.** This method decomposes the application into modular, independent services that interact through well-defined service contracts.

Cloud computing requires the infrastructure to be in place to support the needs of continuous integration and continuous delivery. To be successful, developers need some fundamental capabilities including achieving resilience, being able to discover reusable services and providing the organization with the ability to scale on demand.

Achieving resilience

It's critical for cloud applications to adhere to a service level guarantee regardless of where their services run. Historically, cloud services relied on virtual machines tied to a specific server environment. But as more cloud services become customer facing, resiliency is imperative. However, with virtual machines (VMs) you cannot assume the VMs or the network services you deploy will be permanent. Too often these VMs will disappear because of a systems error. The consequences can be significant since without any warning your applications may not gracefully shutdown. While it may be possible to restart the VM, the problem may not be resolved. This means you have to architect for failure and assume that any services you interact with could disappear at any given time.

Discovering reusable services

Since cloud native applications are designed to take advantage of containers and microservices, it is imperative to be able to locate services that have been vetted so that they can be used in other applications. Therefore, any services your applications interact with need to be found, usually from a runtime registry.

Requiring scalability

One of the most important benefits of the cloud is the ability to scale your infrastructure as your needs change. With traditional applications hosted in the cloud, the need for resources is typically determined at deployment time. However, as you move to a cloud native approach it is critical to scale horizontally - often called scaling out. The continuous development and deployment environment requires horizontal scalability to function effectively.

While there are a number of orchestration platforms, Kubernetes has emerged as the de facto standard. For more details about Kubernetes, take a look at Chapter 4. In a Kubernetes-based cloud environment where clustering is foundational, horizontal scaling is mandatory for performance of servers and nodes because it adds more instances to spread and balance the load.

Moving from VMs to cloud native

Cloud computing has evolved significantly over the past decade making it easier for developers to quickly gain access to compute and storage capabilities and create a platform for applications creation and deployment. Traditionally, developers have relied on virtual machines as a technique to create cloud services. In essence, virtual machine software makes a single system act as though it were a discrete collection of independent services. However, virtual machines sit on a layer of software including the operating system, middleware and tools, which makes the VM more complex and slows down the process of continuous integration and rapid applications development.

Creating innovation

Optimizing business value means that applications can take advantage of the distributed, scalable architecture the cloud platform provides in order to offer the highest levels of flexibility, scalability and reusability. For a cloud native application, this is where true innovation lies today.

The cloud native application fully exploits the benefits of cloud technology. It is important to recognize that a cloud native application is not defined by where it is running, but rather how it is built. Because a cloud native environment is based on containerization, it is not physically tied to a specific hardware or operating system. Therefore, cloud native applications are designed to work on a variety of cloud environment.

Open source cloud native applications

If you are going to adapt an agile continuous integration and continuous delivery model for your cloud applications, you need to explore innovative tools and techniques that apply to the full lifecycle of applications creation and deployment. Most of the most important innovations in native cloud tools are based on open source technologies from a vibrant community of contributors. For example, the Cloud Native Computing Foundation, focused on projects designed to create and deploy cloud-native applications and services. The foundation's work has resulted in a number of projects (completed or underway), including Helm (for package management), Harbor (a registry), and of course, Kubernetes (for container orchestration).

One only has to look at companies including Facebook, Netflix and Twitter that must constantly change their platforms to adapt to changing user expectations. All these companies take advantage of continuous delivery, immutable containers and microservices to help achieve the elastic scaling capabilities needed to cater for an unpredictable competitive landscape. The sense of urgency is palpable: adapt quickly or die.

Indeed, Netflix's transition to cloud native when it spun off a part of its business from the physical DVD rentals to a profitable streaming service is a case in point. After the company suffered from a massive database corruption episode, the service was out of commission for three days. As a result, the company determined it needed a new architecture that could utilize the horizontal scaling capabilities of a public cloud and a microservices approach to software development.

Differentiating cloud native applications

Traditionally, many organizations considered the cloud because of lower costs – a valid reason, but a limited one. Prior to being able to build cloud native applications, cost savings was often the main driver. Cloud native applications enable businesses to shift from focusing exclusively on cost savings to being able to quickly build applications that bring a competitive advantage. In a highly fluid business environment, this is critical for success.

Cloud native applications are built to run on hardware that is modular and automated, allowing them to become both resilient and predictable. Performance and scalability become important benefits, resulting from the ability to flexibly deploy workloads wherever they need to be.

Traditional applications simply do not offer those benefits.

The technologies used to create and deploy cloud-enabled applications (covered in more detail in the next section of this chapter) provide an abstraction layer away from the underlying software and hardware infrastructures, including the operating system. Developers can focus exclusively on building their applications without the need to deal with dependencies of the underlying infrastructure. By creating applications that do not rely on the underlying infrastructure, development and deployment teams can deploy applications on the most pragmatic platform.

Well-designed cloud native applications automatically provision and configure tasks and can dynamically allocate resources based on application requirements. This automation is one way that scalability can be achieved and how applications can balance themselves to prevent failures.

While DevOps methodologies are not unique to cloud native application development, DevOps is a necessary component of cloud native applications. The collaboration associated with a DevOps approach involves the integration of processes, tools, and of course, developers. DevOps creates an environment in which software can be written, tested and released quickly and as often as needed with minimum disruption. As we noted previously, DevOps can be the enabler of an organization's CI/CD goals because the software modules created for a cloud native application can be released continuously and in an automated fashion.

The foundation of microservices

To create true native cloud applications requires different thinking, collaboration and manageability approaches. Cloud-enabled applications are designed to be modular, distributed, deployed and managed in an automated way. These characteristics require technologies that go beyond what was typical for the development of traditional software.

The technologies start with an architectural style that incorporates the modularity concept. Cloud native applications are built as a collection of multiple, independent microservices. Each of these microservices is designed to support one discrete, bounded piece of application functionality. Although these microservices are independent, they can be linked together in a coordinated fashion to provide all the functionality the application is intended to deliver.

Microservices provide a number of significant benefits:

- Application development is simplified since each microservice is built to serve a specific and limited purpose. Small development teams can focus on writing code for narrowly defined and more easily understood functions.

- Code changes will be smaller and less complex than with a complex integrated application, making it easier and faster to make changes, whether to fix a problem or to upgrade a service with new requirements.

- Scalability - both up and down - makes it simpler to deploy an additional instance of a service or change that service as needs evolve.

- Microservices are fully tested and validated. When new applications leverage existing microservices, developers can assume the integrity of the new application without the need for continual testing.

The imperative to manage microservices

It's easy to see how microservices can help organizations fully exploit the advantages of the cloud. Microservices are designed to be packaged within containers that are then managed through orchestration services. These orchestration services are needed to manage both process and logic as well as data services. In effect, it is a game of numbers – there are often many microservices, and many instances of microservices that are distributed over many systems. Keeping track and consistently documenting of all of these microservices is a challenge. In Chapter 4, we will address the role that Kubernetes plays in managing microservices.

Supporting technologies for cloud-enabled applications

Cloud-enabled software is generally built using containers, which are software elements packaged with everything needed to execute it - an application's code, the runtime environment, required system tools and libraries and settings. Each container runs in a virtualized environment, but completely isolated from the underlying infrastructure.

A container's abstraction makes it possible to port the service to virtually any system. Containers can be spun up or down based on the user load present at any given time. Clearly, containers are a critical foundational element for building and running cloud-enabled applications.

The role of APIs

Of course, in a highly distributed environment composed of microservices, the ability to communicate between services is critical if the benefits of the cloud are to be fully realized. Application programming interfaces (APIs) serve this purpose and have special applicability to the cloud. In fact, they are the mode of communication among microservices and containers using inter-process communication mechanisms.

APIs have been used extensively in the past for communicating with and connecting various IT assets. They are an important connectivity mechanism for the way services are combined to create an application. In addition, at the Infrastructure as a Service (IaaS) level, APIs are used to provide control and distribution mechanisms for resources such as provisioning, for example. At the application level Software as a Service (SaaS) APIs furnish the ability to connect applications with the underlying infrastructure and, when applicable, cloud resources.

APIs become even more critical when one or more cloud providers are involved. In these multi-cloud cases, your API strategy needs to consider the APIs provided by the cloud providers themselves to allow connectivity and communication with their clouds. Many cloud providers are offering more generic (e.g., HTTP) integration capabilities to make it easy for their customers to integrate and access resources.

With microservices typically deployed in the form of containers, the inter-process communication mechanisms used with microservices are different from traditional applications. Because the microservices are more granular, so too are the APIs. This means client data requests may span a number of microservices, requiring the request to follow a "one-to-many" form of interaction.

A number of API platforms, including API management platforms, are available today that address a variety of needs in the cloud. Choosing the right API platform involves a careful assessment of the application environment.

Setting the stage for cloud-enabled applications

For many organizations, enabling applications for the cloud is a journey, which in many cases begins with the obvious step of setting a vision and goals. Establishing business objectives is an important first step, since there is a tendency to look at exciting technologies before figuring out direction and what specific business goals need to be achieved. Additionally, planning should involve all stakeholders – corporate management, IT, partners and even customers.

Once goals are set, a team of development, security and operations personnel needs to be created that can take the cloud application implementation to the next level using a DevSecOps approach. One of the first decisions this team will face is which workloads represent the highest priority in terms of cloud-enablement – and this holds true for both legacy and new, more modern applications some of which need to be created. The team will need to consider a number of factors, including business criticality and technical complexity and difficulty. Overall, workloads need to be assessed and prioritized based on business requirements and financial return on investment considerations.

Business services will then need to be defined based on the required application functionality. Decomposing an application into a set of microservices follows no set rules. In general, however, examining the specific services and how they interact "outward" (to customers and other stakeholders), and "inward" (with internal and back office services), and dividing functionality will be based on the most efficient way to orchestrate these interactions. Interacting with back end systems is particularly important, since in some cases, containerization may not be a viable option.

There are a variety of container platforms available in the marketplace – some are open source. In addition, some container platforms are offered by vendors who add value in terms of ease of use and scalability. The careful examination of current and future needs will play into determining the right platform to use.

Finally, the role of operations will change where cloud-enabled applications prevail. We've seen that cloud enablement can add complexity and pose management challenges, but also create great opportunity to exploit the cloud. Kubernetes as a management and orchestration system for cloud native applications built with containers is a way to effectively get the most out of a distributed, modularized application implementation.

Chapter 4

The Power of Kubernetes

Inside
- »   Understanding the importance of containers
- »   Defining the value of microservices
- »   The advantages of Kubernetes
- »   The technical building blocks of Kubernetes

Kubernetes has become the industry standard cloud platform supported by every major cloud provider. Based on an open source architecture, this container orchestration platform provides a powerful foundation. In this chapter we will explore why Kubernetes is so important and the elements that are included to support portability and manageability of a container environment. We will define containers and the role Docker and microservices play in the overall container environment. Finally, we will get into the details about the elements of the Kubernetes platform.

Defining containers

A container is an image based on a lightweight executable collection of software elements that are packaged with all of the software needed to run the workload, regardless of the environment of origin. One of the benefits of containers is that they provide a software environment that brings all the elements needed to run a piece of code together into a filing system.

The container can include the runtime services, system tools and libraries. These services are brought together into a filing system so that they can be installed on a server or on the cloud. The benefit of the container is that it ensures the software will consistently and predictably run on any environment. In addition, a container makes it easy to create a self-healing and auto-scaling process.

Unlike a virtual machine, the container does not require an operating system, and software environment services. On the other hand, a virtual machine communicates through a hypervisor on a shared physical hardware environment. A VM must contain its own operating system and does not get direct access to its host's resources. Therefore, a container has a much smaller footprint when compared to a virtual machine. Rather than requiring a copy of the operating system, a container utilizes the host's operating system.

Available for both Linux- and Windows-based applications, containerized software will always run the same way, regardless of the environment. Containers isolate software from its surroundings such as differences between development and staging environments, and helps reduce conflicts between teams running different software on the same infrastructure.

The value of microservices

Before we get into the details of containers and Kubernetes, it is important to understand the importance of microservices - one of the architectures that is core to the value of containers.

The idea of creating business services without dependencies has been the goal of modern software development for decades. In the past, developers tried to create small software elements that could be grouped together to create larger applications. In many cases, these services were simply too numerous and too granular. The alternative was to encapsulate existing monolithic code as a service. Neither of these approaches worked well.

In contrast, microservices is a process of developing applications that consist of code that is independent of each other and of the underlying developing platform. Once created, each microservice runs a unique process and communicates through well-defined and standardized APIs. These services are defined in a catalog so that developers can more easily locate the right service and understand the governance rules for usage.

To create an application, a variety of microservices need to be managed and linked together. Microservices are designed to be linked together to create a business process. Because these services are modular, it is much easier for developers to change a service as the business process changes.

Microservices separate business logic functions into smaller application services that can communicate over standard HTTP. In essence, microservices isolates faults and exceptions so that if one service fails, the entire application doesn't fail. An example of a microservice is authentication. A team could build, test and publish an access and identity microservice. The access and identity microservice could then be utilized across teams rather than each project needing to develop their own authentication method.

With every benefit comes some complexities. A group of microservices must be logically linked together and orchestrated. This requires overhead to support the orchestration. The solution to the complexity of orchestration and management of microservices is Dockers and Kubernetes. We will discuss both offerings in our next sections.

The role of Docker

Docker, an open source container technology was introduced in 2013 and has become the de facto container standard. At the core of Docker's open source container technology, is an engine that helps developers create, ship and run the application containers. Docker provides an environment to support services including a registry that stores, distributes and shares container images. These containers can run on any deployment environment including on-premise data centers and private clouds as well as virtual machines and public clouds. Unlike a virtual machine, the container does not require an operating system. Docker enables developers to create, ship and run the application containers. The resulting Docker images files are very small which helps reduce overhead and improves performance.

The benefits of Docker include:

- **Isolate processes into their own namespace.** Docker makes it easier to start and stop processes and have persistence within the container.

- **Registry of images that are managed in an image cache.** Docker offers a consistent way to manage images so they can be built on the fly and then be automatically pushed into the registry.

- **Configuration management complexity is made easier.**

- **Build management** helps developers spin up a virtual image in a simple and fast way.

Defining Kubernetes

If microservices are the content, and docker containers are the wrapper, then Kubernetes is the way the containers are orchestrated and managed in a hybrid cloud environment. Google open sourced the Kubernetes project in 2015. Today, Kubernetes builds upon a decade and a half of experience that Google has with running production workloads at scale, combined with best-of-breed ideas and practices from the community.

Kubernetes is a portable, extensible open source platform for managing containerized workloads and services. Kubernetes is optimized to support all infrastructure platforms, from virtual machines to bare-metal. The technology is designed to support both stateful and stateless applications. Kubernetes abstracts each individual infrastructure platform and supports cluster federation and auto-balancing across hybrid clouds. Kubernetes facilitates both declarative configuration and automation.

Because Kubernetes has such a large open source contributing community, the platforms supports a large and rapidly growing ecosystem of tools and services including Prometheus for monitoring, Istio for service meshes, Kaniko for building containers and Open Tracing for distributed tracing.

One of the benefits of Kubernetes is that it standardizes the orchestration of container services. It provides a platform for automating the development, scaling and operation of systems across a cluster of hosts. In addition, some of the primary benefits of Kubernetes include:

- Standardized way to build, package, deploy and run applications of any language

- Portability across multiple cloud providers and the ability to avoid vendor lock-in

- Horizontal auto scaling so that additional pods are created as application demand increases

- High availability through continual health checks to make ensure that nodes and containers are operating as expected

- Automated rollouts to updated applications or its configurations without causing downtime

Kubernetes provides tools for application deployment, service discovery, scheduling, updating, maintenance and scaling. Kubernetes is extensible so that it can support a variety of use cases across many different implementations. Therefore, Kubernetes is architected to sit on top of the physical infrastructure.

Like most platforms, Kubernetes has a built-in set of rudimentary tools that allow you to monitor your servers. The term "built-in" may be a little bit of an overstatement. Given the extensible nature of Kubernetes, it is possible to add additional components to gain visibility into Kubernetes. For example, Custom Resource Definitions (CDR) are the way to extend Kubernetes and still leverage capabilities from the platform. CDR extends the API so that additional services can be added to the cluster.

Before we get into the details of the physical Kubernetes clusters, it is instructive to understand the logical or application view of Kubernetes clusters. Figure 4-1 shows how a Kubernetes deployment is organized in a hierachical fashion.

For example, all of the containers run inside of pods which are a set of one or more containers that reside together. The pods sit behind services like load balancing. Furthermore, services are scaled by ReplicaSets that can spin up or delete pods as they are needed. The namespace is a virtual cluster that can include one or more services.

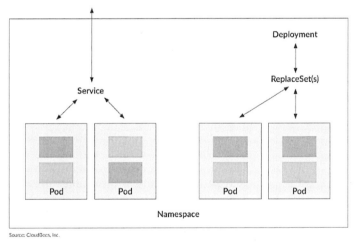

Source: CloudBees, Inc.

Figure 4-1: The logical view of how a Kubernetes cluster
is deployed

Elements of Kubernetes

To support a variety of environments and requirements, Kubernetes includes a variety of services that enable the orchestration of containers. In this section, we will take a close look at each of these elements that is important for creating a sophisticated continuous integration/continuous delivery (CI/CD) environment.

Master node

One of the main functions of Kubernetes is to manage workloads. On a conceptual level, Kubernetes is made up of a bunch of nodes with different roles. The control plane on the master node(s) consists of the API Server, the Controller Manager and Scheduler(s). The Master Node is designed to make these workloads highly available. Therefore, the master node manages an abstracted control plane that includes the API server, controller manager server, and etcd (we will define each of these elements below). Think of the master node as the stage manager for all the services that are needed to manage containerized applications. The master node manages application services across a set of containers or hosts and provides mechanisms for deployment, maintenance and application scaling. A Kubernetes cluster consists of one or more masters and a set of nodes. The master can be configured to support High Availability (HA) so there is no single point of failure. In addition, the master is responsible for managing all of the nodes within the Kubernetes cluster and then schedules pods to run on those nodes.

Worker node

The master node handles and manages the cluster but it does not actually run any containers. Instead, the worker node runs the Docker container. Depending on the design of the cluster, a worker node can be either a virtual machine or a physical machine. Each worker node includes all of the services needed to run pods (or a cluster of containers). It is managed by the master node. These nodes do not have a public IP address and therefore process data on the node and report resources to the master node.

API server

The API Server manages the entire cluster by processing REST operations, validates them, and updates the corresponding objects in etcd. One important function of the API Server is to authentication and authorization of the interactions with the API clients.

The Kubernetes API server is designed to validate and configure the data for pods, services and replication controllers. In addition, the API server assigns pods (or a group of containers) so they can be deployed as a unit on the same host) to the cluster of nodes. At this point, the API server synchronizes the container group information with service configuration. The API Server is the central manager that communicates directly with distributed storage and can manipulate the state of services.

Etcd storage

Managing clusters across distributed systems is complicated. Etcd is an open source distributed key value store that provides shared configuration and service discovery for container Linux clusters. Etcd replicates the state data across all nodes in the cluster, preventing a single node failure from bringing down the whole group. Etcd runs on each machine in a cluster and gracefully handles leader election during network partitions and the loss of the current leader. Etcd stores the persistent master state while other components watch etcd for changes to bring themselves into the desired state.

In order to asynchronously monitor changes to keys, etcd includes a watch feature. If a key is changed, the watcher is notified so that the right business logic is updated to its desired state.

Scheduler

This component watches the API for unscheduled pods, then finds a machine for them to run and informs the API server of the best choice. The job of the scheduler is to make sure that resources needed are available. For example, there might be low memory or not enough disk space. The scheduler can look for another pod that can handle the task.

Controller manager

The controller manager server watches etcd for changes to replication controller objects and then uses the API to enforce the desired state. Several such processes create a cluster with one active leader at a time.

Kubelet

The kubelet is the lowest level component in Kubernetes and is responsible for knowing what is running on each machine. Therefore, the kubelet has a single task: it keeps a set of containers running. It is basically an agent on the node that actually starts and stops containers and communicates with the Docker engine at a host level. The kubelet interacts with the API Server and watches to make sure that pods are bound to its node and are running. It is present on every node in a Kubernetes cluster: both master and worker nodes. It talks with the API server. It only manages containers created by Kubernetes. The kubelet does not manage containers that are not created by Kubernetes.

Kube-proxy

The kube-proxy daemon runs on each worker node as a simple network proxy and load balancer for the services on that node. The kube proxy itself redirects traffic to a specific services and pods. It is in regular communication with the API server.

Kubectl

Kubectl is a command line tool for communicating with a Kubernetes API. This tool is used to create, inspect, update and delete Kubernetes objects. It includes an agent that runs on each node in the cluster to help ensure that containers are running in a pod.

Why Kubernetes is key to CI/CD in the cloud

It is clear that Kubernetes is an extremely powerful platform for creating and managing services and containers in a standard way. The power of both containers and microservices can help organizations respond quickly to changing business requirements.

Chapter 5

Meet Jenkins X

Inside

- » Understanding Jenkins X
- » The technical architecture of Jenkins X
- » Using GitOps for promotion
- » The business benefits of Jenkins X

While containers have the potential to dramatically simplify and speed up the development of new applications, they also bring on a new set of complexities. Indeed, with Kubernetes emerging as the de facto standard for container orchestration, its popularity spawned hundreds of open source tools for developers. Many of these tools are powerful and give developers multiple options.

However, with all this flexibility, it is difficult to track and manage developers using a wide variety of tools. In many cases, developers choose their favored tools, and businesses end up with dozens of overlapping tools. It becomes a challenge for organizations who want to standardize their tools to improve quality, speed, consistency and collaboration.

To help solve the challenge of disparate tools, Jenkins X provides a technique to abstract Kubernetes orchestration by including the best of breed tools in an opinionated platform. Jenkins X packages these tools and automates the processes, so developers can focus on writing code and building the application. In this chapter, we will explore the elements of Jenkins X; in Chapter 6, we will cover how to get started with Jenkins X.

What is Jenkins X?

Jenkins X is an open source project designed to help accelerate the creation of cloud native applications by hiding the complexities of Kubernetes for CI and CD services. It comes with all the automation capabilities required by developers so that they can focus on writing the application code. For example, Jenkins X automates releases with semantic versions and creates artifacts, Docker images and helm charts. It also automatically promotes versioned artifacts across the environment via GitOps.

Jenkins X automates the processes by providing a wrapper around Kubernetes. Jenkins X can leverage any source code and it doesn't care if you are using a traditional middleware. In other words, Jenkins X simply doesn't care what services are running under the covers. Jenkins X provides a platform that enables the developer to preview the environment. Team members can review changes before they are committed into production. The result is that testing is performed throughout the development process. The architecture of Jenkins X allows it to work seamlessly with any third party cloud including Amazon AWS, Microsoft Azure, Google Cloud, Red Hat OpenShift, or IBM Cloud.

The importance of microservices

The world of application development has moved from an era of writing large, monolithic applications to building applications made up of individual containerized microservices.

The biggest challenges with containers are managing, scaling and load balancing while also making sure they run as intended. As the complexity of your environment increases, you can quickly have thousands of containers that need to be consistently managed. This is where Kubernetes steps in. Kubernetes is a container orchestration, management and automation platform. However, like other platforms, Kubernetes requires specialized knowledge on how to work within the environment. As we discussed in Chapter 4, Kubernetes is a complex cloud container architecture that requires automation to support a CI/CD solution.

What makes Jenkins X different than other options to support CI/CD in the cloud? Jenkins X is an opinionated platform. Rather than dealing with complexities at the code level, Jenkins X selects a set of core services and tools that are pre-installed and wired together so that developers can more easily begin developing applications.

Jenkins X Sits on the Shoulders of Jenkins

Jenkins X began where Jenkins left off. Jenkins was an open source project developed in 2004 and released in 2005 on *java.net* well before the cloud became the development platform of choice. Jenkins helped automate the non-human part of the software development process, with continuous integration and facilitating technical aspects of continuous delivery.

The project, originally called Hudson was renamed Jenkins in 2011. The Jenkins community has become very active. Over the last ten years, more and more developers rely on Jenkins as a foundation for on premises continuous integration and continuous deployment for their applications.

Jenkins X provides the same foundation of automation and extensibility that has made Jenkins so important to developers.

Jenkins X architecture

Jenkins X automates the installation, configuration, and upgrade tasks for a variety of important development, deployment, container and security tools. It includes three important elements to help accelerate the DevOps pipeline: Helm, Prow and Secrets. In this section we will discuss these important tools and technologies.

The continuous automation imperative

Jenkins X performs the backend automation so that developers can begin creating applications without first setting up the environment by hand. In general, rapid, reliable and repeatable delivery of cloud native applications require developers to be cognizant of:

- CI/CD (principles, pipelines, tools, and technology)

- Cloud native concepts (architecture/microservices, technology, principles etc)

- Containers

- Kubernetes/container orchestration

It may take weeks or even months for a team of developers to teach themselves about these topics and then build the applications. Instead, Jenkins X provides developers and small teams a guided solution for delivering cloud native apps on Kubernetes using CI/CD practices.

A key component to Jenkins X is automation throughout the platform. Jenkins X is designed to continuously automate every aspect of Kubernetes from the installation and configuration of tools to keeping individual tools current. Jenkins X includes a single `jx` command line that is the entry point for getting started to create a Kubernetes cluster. The environment is architected so that each team has its own instance of Jenkins X. With these individual instances, each team is able to see their own pipelines in the user interface. This approach means that each team has its own Kubernetes-built pods (individual or multiple containers). In this way, teams can operate at their own pace and don't have to line up behind the entire organization's application pipeline.

Core elements of Jenkins X and supported tools

As an opinionated platform, Jenkins X contains a number of elements designed to help accelerate CI/CD on Kubernetes. These elements include:

Helm. A package manager for Kubernetes that allows teams to more easily install and upgrade applications. Helm uses Helm Charts to help developers define, install and upgrade Kubernetes applications.

Prow. Prow is a collection of utilities used to interact with Git events and schedule build engines. Components include a scalable webhook event handler, automated pull request merger and many plugins to aid a developer's experience.

Secrets. Most applications contain configuration files that handle passwords and other confidential information in the completed application. Jenkins X con tains a helm wrapper called helm secrets. The helm secrets wrapper contains all of the needed components in a single package.

In addition to the core elements, Jenkins X automates the installation, configuration and updates to a variety of open source tools such as:

Skaffold. Skaffold is a command line tool that facilitates continuous development for Kubernetes applications. With Skaffold, developers can iterate an application's source code locally while having it continually updated and ready for validation or testing in their local or remote Kubernetes clusters.

Jenkins. Jenkins is an open source continuous integration software tool written in the Java programming language for testing and reporting on isolated changes in a larger code base in real time. The software enables developers to find and solve defects in a code base rapidly and to automate testing of their builds.

Monocular. Monocular is a user interface designed to discover and run Helm charts.

Nexus. Nexus is a dependency cache for Nodejs and Java applications designed to improve build times.

Docker. Dockers are open source containers.

ChartMuseum. ChartMuseum is a registry for publishing Helm charts.

KSync. KSync is a tool that synchronizes files between a local system and a Kubernetes cluster.

The native support and automation surrounding these tools is designed to allow developers the ability to focus on building applications and creating high-quality code rather than focusing on individual tools.

Understanding GitOps and environment promotion

GitOps is an iteration of a DevOps process designed for cloud native with a focus on Kubernetes. Code managed in Git, makes it easier to track and recover when managed independently of Kubernetes. Continuous delivery approaches for Kubernetes often rely on technologies such as Jenkins.

The value of GitOps is the ability to collaborate in a declarative environment so that the multiple components within a microservices environment can be managed.

GitOps enables the developers to manage and monitor all of the applications and the entire cloud native stack. With GitOps it is much easier for the developer to learn and manage complex Kubernetes clusters.

One of the greatest benefits of GitOps is that it acts a unified "source of the truth." Version control, history, peer review and rollbacks all are managed within the GitOps environment.

This is important when it comes to Jenkins X.

As already mentioned, within Jenkins X, each team gets their own environment. An environment is a place to deploy code and each environment maps to a separate namespace in Kubernetes so that they are isolated from each other and can be managed independently. GitOps manages the environments and performs the promotion.

What does promotion mean? Each environment gets its own Git Repository to store the entire environment-specific configuration together with a list of all the applications and their version and configuration. Promotion of new application versions results in the following:

- Pull Request is created for the configuration change that triggers the CI pipeline tests on the Environment along with code review and approval.

- The Pull Request is merged with the release pipeline for the environment that updates the applications running in that environment by applying the helm chart metadata from the git repository.

Streamlining software development while improving quality

Businesses and the developers supporting changing business needs want to adopt lean practices and processes so that development is streamlined. The emergence of the cloud means that development processes must be fast and practical. While at the outset this may sound straightforward, in a highly distributed multi-cloud computing environment there are many moving parts.

The new world of software creation requires that software is developed as modular components that are constantly being tested and used in a variety of situations. These software elements have to be tested, integrated with other services and then put into deployment.

However, this is not a static process. Developers are required to ensure that changes and new services work as anticipated and don't create new problems. It is incumbent on the development team to create a DevOps environment that can cope with complexity and change. Moving forward, development teams have to work as one with the operations group in order to create new cloud native applications that scale and change as new services are added.

Why businesses need Jenkins X

Businesses across the globe are increasingly relying on cloud computing, and not just for compute, storage or software as a service. Rather, technologists are looking at cloud services as a way to rapidly innovate their software without constraints. With cloud infrastructure and services, developers can experiment without putting their company's business at risk. Developers have the freedom to innovate without being limited by existing legacy applications and infrastructure. Likewise, business leaders can develop new business models, pilot them in near real time, fail without consequences, and create innovation to develop new revenue streams.

So, why does an organization need Jenkins X to achieve these business and technical goals? It is increasingly clear that both Kubernetes and microservices help enable a continuous integration and continuous development and deployment environment. The irony is that speed and flexibility come at a cost. You need to be able to be supported by a set of frameworks and models that allow you to move fast but in a predictable and manageable way. Not every organization can afford to hire developers deeply knowledgeable about advanced DevOps environments. Rather, it is important to provide developers with the tools that can make it easier for them to take advantage of the latest innovations in software development in the cloud. This is where Jenkins X comes in.

Jenkins X allows developers to focus on building excellent user experiences and innovative applications rather than creating underlying environments that do not create business differentiation. Smart businesses want their developers to focus as much time as possible on creating great applications rather non-differentiating tooling.

The commercialization of Jenkins X open source

Like Jenkins, Jenkins X is an open source offering and enjoys a growing community. As we have seen with other open source tools and environments, the technology becomes more common in production applications in which IT leaders demand enterprise-level features and direct support.

When open source tools are used in business critical applications, many businesses have a requirement for enterprise support. While open source software projects have frequent updates and are community supported, they typically require sophisticated developers to "go it alone" when they run into new challenges or are trying to integrate the open source tool into their existing environment. By contrast, enterprise-supported versions are

differentiated with the following features, provided with
the software code:

- Guaranteed service level agreements (SLAs)

- Support contracts

- Testing before new updates are integrated

- Higher levels of security testing and patches

- Accountability through enterprise contract

How should a developer get started?

The goal of this chapter was to help you understand the
value of leveraging Kubernetes combined with Jenkins X
to simplify your approach to building cloud native applications. As you have seen in this chapter, Jenkins X automates many of the tasks required to begin using Kubernetes to create a new generation of applications. These
applications are dynamic and require frequent updates,
while also adding new services that have to be continuously tested and managed as customer needs evolve. In
the next chapter, we will delve into what it means to put
Kubernetes supported by Jenkins X into action.

Chapter 6

Kicking the Tires of Jenkins X

Inside
- » Recognizing the value of Kubernetes
- » Getting started with Jenkins X
- » Deploying Jenkins X in the enterprise

Jenkins X is a critical tool that offers developers a level of abstraction for building and deploying cloud native apps with Kubernetes. In this chapter we will discuss what it means to put Jenkins X into practice. We'll start with the basics.

Kubernetes adoption

As we discussed in Chapter 4, Kubernetes has become the de facto standard for managing and orchestrating containers and is changing everything when it comes to developing cloud native applications. As Kubernetes becomes embraced by a large number of vendors and customers, there is a growing ecosystem of tools available for the environment. How does a developer know which tools to select? How does a developer bring these tools together to be able to create a project that meets the needs of their CI/CD pipeline? As we discussed in Chapter 5, Jenkins X was designed to bring together the best of breed tools into a framework to help you move quickly in developing, testing, implementing and deploying applications for the cloud.

Getting started

When developers begin working with Kubernetes, they are often confronted with a daunting level of complexity. To start using Kubernetes, developers need to spend time learning about the platform and its capabilities. Jenkins X helps to flatten the learning curve of Kubernetes by adding automation and hiding the complexities of creating a Kubernetes environment so that developers can get started quickly. So, how do you get started? To begin the process of using Jenkins X requires installing a number of programming constructs. In the next section, we will discuss the steps in using Jenkins X to establish your environment.

Setting up a Kubernetes cluster

Your first step is to download and install the jx command line tool. Depending on your operating system you will use a different set of instruction. The jx command will automatically create a new Kubernetes cluster, installing required local dependencies and provisions on the Jenkins X platform. These clusters work across a variety of cloud providers environments including Amazon AWS, Microsoft Azure, Oracle Cloud, Google Cloud, as well as custom Kubernetes clusters. If you would like to see a demo of the command take a look at this link:

https://jenkins-x.io/demos/create_cluster/

Creating a quickstart

A quickstart provides the developer with a command line interface (CLI) for creating a Kubernetes cluster. When you want to begin creating a new application, it is sensible to use a quickstart, a pre-made application rather than starting from scratch. Jenkins X includes a curated set of quickstart applications that can be accessed through the jx create quickstart command. ($ jx create quickstart). You are then prompted for a list of quickstarts to choose from. Once you have chosen the project to create and given it a name the following tasks are automated:

- ✓ Creates a new application from the quickstart in a sub directory.
- ✓ Adds your source code into a git repository.
- ✓ Creates a remote git repository on a git service, such as GitHub.
- ✓ Pushes your code to the remote git service.
- ✓ Adds default files:
  - ✓ Dockerfile to build your application as a docker image.
  - ✓ Jenkinsfile to implement the CI/CD pipeline.
  - ✓ Helm chart to run your application inside Kubernetes.

- ✓ Registers a webhook on the remote git repository to your team's Jenkins.
- ✓ Adds the git repository to your team's Jenkins.
- ✓ Triggers the first pipeline.

Once you have created a quickstart, you can use either jx create spring or jx import. At this point the Jenkins X build packs are used to:

- Find the right language pack. A few language pack examples include PHP, Ruby, Swift, and Python along with many others.

- The language pack is then used to default these files if they don't already exist:

  o Dockerfile to package the application as a docker image.

  o Jenkinsfile to implement the CI/CD pipelines using declarative pipeline as code.

  o Helm charts to deploy the application on Kubernetes and to implement Preview Environments.

Importing a project

You may already have source code that you want to import into Jenkins X. In order to execute on the import process, you can use the `jx import` command (`cd my-cool-app $ jx import`). This command will perform the following actions:

- ✓ Add your source code into the git repository.

- ✓ Create a remote git repository on a git service, such as GitHub.

- ✓ Push your code to the remote git service.

- ✓ Add any required files to your project (Dockerfiles, Jenkinsfiles, helm charts).

- ✓ Register a webhook on the remote git repository to your team's Jenkins.

- ✓ Add the git repository to your team's Jenkins.

- ✓ Trigger the first pipeline.

Build packs and overriding values

Jenkins X offers a number of different kinds of build packs for projects including Go, Node.js, and Spring Boot. In essence, build packs are quickstarts for creating Kubernetes clusters.

While it is typical to allow Jenkins X to automatically perform the standard setup, there are times when you will need to override a pre-set configuration.

The override function is a feature of Helm that allows developers to override standard configurations. For example, you may have an application running in a staging environment. If it is in this staging environment, you do not need the application to be highly available. However, when you are ready to move that application into production it must be highly available so you will want to change the availability level. This overriding will be done within GitOps (discussed in Chapter 5). There are other situations when you need to be able to allocate more memory or storage space. However, these overrides are the exception and should be used sparingly.

Enterprise deployments

As we've discussed, the goal of Jenkins X is to provide developers with a quick way to start building cloud native applications and getting started with Kubernetes. Developers have to understand how to promote applications into production using GitOps. As you recall from Chapter 5, promoting an application means to either automatically or manually moving the application along your pipeline to the next stage. To support the needs of enterprise teams, Jenkins X includes a number of features, including preview environments and liveness and keepalives.

Preview environments

A preview environment is one of the important features of Jenkins X because it allows developers to automatically get feedback on changes made before it is merged into the master.

Liveness and keepalives

In Kubernetes when you start up a cluster, this function will check to see if the pod (a group of one or more containers) is ready to accept traffic. Kubernetes will use a liveness probe to determine if the pod is ready to run. Once the pod is running, keepalive makes sure it is still running. If the pod is not running, liveness will create a new pod.

Jenkins X and the value of abstraction

This chapter provided you with the ability to get started quickly with Jenkins X and Kubernetes. In truth Kubernetes out of the box is incredibly difficult to work with. For developers, it can take a long time to understand the basics – and even longer to become productive. Developers who have begun their journey with Jenkins X don't have to know the underlying details of Kubernetes before they can start delivering value. And, better yet, they can avoid common mistakes that could delay them from developing cloud native applications fast.

Chapter 7

Resources for Getting Started with Jenkins X

Inside

- » Increase your knowledge on continuous integration, continuous delivery and DevOps
- » Preparing to build cloud native applications
- » Getting help with Kubernetes
- » Learning more about Jenkins X

Jenkins X provides an abstracted platform to support the needs of developers to create cloud native applications leveraging Kubernetes. In this book, we have provided insights into the capabilities of Kubernetes and the Jenkins X environment to support developers as they enter the world of DevOps and continuous integration and continuous delivery services.

In this chapter, we provide links to resources that will help your teams get started.

Continuous integration, continuous delivery and DevOps resources

What is DevOps?
https://www.cloudbees.com/devops

Building continuous delivery pipelines with Jenkins
https://www.cloudbees.com/resource/whitepaper/easily-build-continuous-delivery-pipelines-jenkins-and-pipe-line-plugin

Business value of Jenkins X
https://www.cloudbees.com/blog/business-value-jen-kins-x-automating-continuous-everything-kubernetes

Master DevOps for software innovation
https://www.cloudbees.com/resource/whitepaper/for-rester-research-report-master-devops-faster-delivery-software-innovation

Cloud native resources

The Cloud Native Computing Foundation offers a wealth of resources on its site:

https://www.cncf.io/

There are a number of other sites that offer assistance including the following:

What are cloud native applications?
https://opensource.com/article/18/7/what-are-cloud-native-apps

Cloud native SIG
https://jenkins.io/sigs/cloud-native/

Kubernetes resources

Before you can move forward, you need to understand Kubernetes as the key system for automating deployment and management of containerized applications. A variety of resources, including documentation, educational, and other relevant content can be found on the Kubernetes.io site:

https://kubernetes.io/

The GitHub development platform also offers some helpful information on both Kubernetes and Jenkins X. Below are some useful links.

Kubernetes on GitHub
https://github.com/kubernetes

Kubernetes basics tutorial
https://kubernetes.io/docs/tutorials/kubernetes-basics/

Serverless Kubernetes
https://www.cloudbees.com/blog/kubernetes-without-servers

Jenkins X on GitHub
https://github.com/jenkins-x

Helm is the package manager for Kubernetes and includes Tiller, the server side implementation of Helm. Here is a link to help you understand and implement Helm:

https://docs.helm.sh/using_helm/

Learn more about Jenkins X

Jenkins
https://jenkins.io/

Jenkins X
https://jenkins-x.io/

Jenkins X project
https://jenkins.io/blog/2018/03/19/introducing-jenkins-x/

Jenkins X on GitHub
https://github.com/jenkins-x/jx

Under the Hood of Jenkins X
https://www.cloudbees.com/blog/under-hood-jenkins-x-cicd-solution-cloud-applications-kubernetes

Below are links to resources featuring James Strachan, CloudBees, Inc.'s distinguished engineer and chief architect of Jenkins X:

Develop fast with an open source microservices platform
https://www.youtube.com/watch?v=QU60XTe4LoM

Implementing CI/CD using Jenkins X on Kubernetes
https://www.youtube.com/watch?v=BF3MhFjvBTU

Using opinionated Kubernetes and Jenkins X for CD
https://www.cloudbees.com/blog/now-devops-radio-james-strachan-introduces-jenkins-x-taking-continuous-delivery-next-level

CloudBees is a proud sponsor of the Jenkins community and we're pleased to provide you with this book to help you on your cloud native journey.

We know it is important to streamline your software delivery processes and leveraging Kubernetes and Jenkins X in your cloud environment is an important first step.

Indeed, Jenkins X is the solution that hides the complexity of Kubernetes and provides you with a well-tested, commercial platform. CloudBees has worked closely with the Jenkins community, with both of us doing the hard work of bringing together the most productive open source tools into a framework that helps your company be successful in the fast-paced world of cloud native software development, testing, deployment and management.

Try the Jenkins X platform to see the difference!
https://jenkins-x.io/getting-started/

For more information from CloudBees:

Getting started with CI/CD and DevOps metrics
https://www.cloudbees.com/get-started

Implementing CI/CD using Jenkins X on Kubernetes
https://www.cloudbees.com/resource/whitepaper/cicd-cloud-native-applications-kubernetes

Using opinionated Kubernetes and Jenkins X for CD
https://www.cloudbees.com/blog/opinionated-kubernetes-and-jenkins-x